AMATEUR
GRAMMATICS

MARIANNE BURGESS

AMATEUR
GRAMMATICS

For my Dad, who encouraged me to write.

CONTENTS

A DIFFICULT CONVERSATION

"Hello Dad it's only me –
How are you today?"

"Who's this?
Can't hear you very well…
Hello – what did you say?"

"It's ME! It is your DAUGHTER –
I promised you a CALL!"

"You WHAT?
A news reporter?
I don't know anything at all!"

Give me strength…

"Dad it's O-N-L-Y M-E;
I thought I'd say H-E-L-L-O!"

"Eh? Who is this calling?
I can't hear – I've got to go!"

"NO WONDER YOU CAN'T HEAR ME,
THE TV'S BLARING OUT!"

"......I've got my telly on –
I'm afraid you'll have to shout!"

"WEAR YOUR BLOODY HEARING AID!
IT'S NOT ROCKET SCIENCE, IS IT?"

"...If that's you my darling daughter –
I can't hear...
YOU'LL HAVE TO VISIT!!"

THE NON-HOLIDAY

(An Ode to Workaholics)

"I'm going to take a holiday"
Declared the workaholic –
"But not for me the sandy beach
Or any fun and frolic
Nor the sprawling countryside,
Or lovely mountain views
And I wouldn't waste my
Hard earned cash
On an island cruise
In fact conventional outings –
I find them quite grotesque…
So this year I'm in the office,
Holidaying at my desk!"

A GREEK TRAGEDY

The scene was set
A sun kissed beach
And skies above so blue;
I walked past
You turned around –
That's when I first saw you.

Our eyes they met
My mouth went dry
You smoothed your black moustache;
You muttered something Greek –
I think I said, I had to dash!

Much later on
That very night
At the local discotheque,
I spied you with a leggy blonde
Wrapped around your neck

I schmoozed on over
To where you sat
(I would not be rejected!)
I missed the chair
Fell in your lap;
The leggy blonde – ejected!

You picked me up
And brushed me down
You led me out the door –
And then we walked
For miles on end
Along the empty shore….

No words needed to convey
The way you made me feel;
When you held me close to you
I knew our love was real…

And so we stood
And viewed the stars
We held each other tight;
Me and my Greek Adonis
Under the pale moonlight

But then you went
And spoiled it all,
One line was all it took –
In broken pigeon English you said;
'Do you want to fuck?'!

THE OLD OAK TREE

The old oak tree
Stood proud and tall
Her branches open wide;
But no-one else could see the pain
That she felt deep inside.

Only yesterday
She was a shelter from the storm –
And offered shade beneath her arms
When the sun became too warm.

Birds would build their nests up high
Amongst the leaves of green,
And the russet autumn colours
Were a marvel to be seen.

Lovers came to etch their names
Deep in the hard old grain;
That saw the seasons come and go,
And endured the wind and rain.

But the poor old oak she knew deep down
Her time was at an end –
Betrayed by those who loved her once,
Who claimed to be her friend...

For in the very spot she stood
Plans were being made
To take away the awesome sight
On which the children played….

Now the pain the old oak felt that day
Lives deep inside of me –
And I feel it every time I hear
It's nothing but a tree…..

A WORKING DAY

6 a.m alarm clock rings
Another working day begins.
Under shower
Blow dry hair
Look for something
Clean to wear.
Run down-stairs
Slice some bread
Make sure that
The cat's been fed.
Glance at clock
Crunch the toast
Grab coat and bag
And stuff to post
Slam the door
Rush down the street
Reach the station
Find a seat
Take out book
Sit and wait
Announcement made
The train is late.

Arrive at work
'Where've you been?'
Boss red in face

Looking mean.
Apologise for being late
Promise to rub clean
My slate.
Deal with post
Answer phones
Hear the clients'
Moans and groans.
Think of what to cook
For tea
Jot down numbers
Sip coffee.

Wait until
It's half past four
Say good-night
Make for the door
Coat in hand
Run down the street
Reach the station
Flop in seat
Take out book
Sit and wait
Announcement made

The train is late…

Arrive at home
'You're finally here!'
Said hubby pouring
Out a beer.

'It's alright love, the train was late'
Devour the food
Upon my plate
Sit on sofa
Watch TV
Is this all
Life holds for me?
Kiss goodnight
Climb in to bed
Puff-up pillow
Lay down head
Think about tomorrow
When –
Today will start
All over again……

NO SUBSTITUTE

I am not a pass-time
While you get over her –
I am not a sounding board
To hear of how you were.
I am not the one to tell
Of how it should have been;
You cannot use these eyes of mine
To reflect what you have seen.
You cannot use these lips I have
And want them to taste the same…
You cannot tear my heart in two,
While you play your selfish game.

ETHIOPIA

Two hollow eyes
Look up at me
From the screen
On my TV
Eyes that see
Only pain and sorrow
Eyes with no hope
For tomorrow….

THE ONE

Let me throw my cloak
Of love around you
And take away
Your pain.

Let me pave your walk
Through life with sunshine
And dry up all
The rain.

Let me be the dawn
For you each morning
The stars in heaven for you
Each night.

Let me be the one to
Hold you close
And tell you everything will be
All right.

Let me be the reason
That you're living –
The reason you
Would die.

Let me be the soul
Your heart has searched for
Let me be the
Reason why.

EXPRESS SERVICE

I parked beside pump no.2
I filled her up with fuel;
I joined the fastest moving queue
Now I'm held up by this fool –
Who thought he'd do the weekly shop
And stood with piled high trolley,
But the bleeping of the scanner stopped –
To cries of 'blast!' and 'golly!'
As the shop assistant tried in vain
To scan his bag of sweets
The fool stood rooted to the spot
Defensive of his treats –
'I'll go and get some help' she said,
And after quite an age –
He was offered something else instead
While we all seethed in rage;
'But I want my pack of sweets!' he cried –
'I know, but they won't scan!'
The Manager came and tried and tried,
To work out a kind of plan...

And the queue was getting long,
And the people were complaining –

This all seemed very wrong,
And outside it started raining…
While all this was taking place
I saw the colour drain
Straight from the fool's anxious face,
As he asked them to refrain –
His memory must have failed
He'd been in another store;
'I bought the sweets from there!' he wailed –
And bolted out the door!
And so the queue quickly dispersed
As I tried hard to repress
The frustration about to burst,
Right there – in Tesco Express;
When I handed her some chewing gum
I'd taken off the rack,
And the cashier looked at me all glum
And said – 'Need any help to pack?'

THE END

Time is running out my friends
Soon we will be no more;
And there won't be any winners
In this bloody war.

The sun that smiled upon us
Is weeping tears of pain –
And from the great clouds up above
There now falls acid rain.

The stars that twinkled in the sky
Are barely but a spark –
And soon they will all fade out,
And earth will just be dark.

We're chopping all the forests up
And trampling down the flowers;
We're killing all the living things
In this world of ours.

If you are up in Heaven God
Then you must be irate –
Why don't you do something to help,
Before it gets too late?

FORBIDDEN FRUIT

Your eyes say that you want me.
My eyes say the same.
A chemical reaction.
That's part of the mating game.
I know that I shouldn't want you
As I'm no longer free –
Why does the taste of forbidden fruit
Keep on tormenting me?

I DON'T LOVE MY CAT
(MORE THAN YOU)

I don't love my cat
More than you;
But she never nags at me
The way you do!
She doesn't keep asking
What's on my mind –
Or say things to me
That are unkind!

I don't love my cat
More than you;
And I don't want to chose
Between you two –
But she loves me
Despite my mood,
And is content
With just a bowl of food!

I don't love my cat
More than you;
But she doesn't get jealous
The way you do!
And she never tells me
That I'm 'obsessed' –
I just want her to have
The very best!

I don't love my cat
More than you;
Please get into bed –
I LOVE YOU, I DO!
You're crazy to think
My cat comes before us;
Let's go to sleep
And stop making a fuss!

I don't love my cat
More than you;
It's just your barmy
Point of view!
Just take your pillow
Your duvet and sheet;
See her curled up on your side –
Ain't she sweet?

I don't love my cat
More than you;
This doesn't require
A judicial review!
Get used to the floor
It's your new habitat –
But don't make a sound please,
You might wake my cat!

HOT SWEATS

My temperature gauge
Is definitely broke,
I've been pouring with sweat
Since the minute I woke…
I am red in the face
And I cannot abate
The inferno within me
That's lying in wait!

And it looks like I've run
A marathon race
When beads of sweat
Take over my face;
Then the heat turns up
And it starts to show –
Like a beacon of light
I'm now all aglow!

Folks cross the road
When they see me approach
All red faced and sweaty –
(For fear of reproach),
The look in their eyes
Tells me they don't trust

That I'm not about
To spontaneously combust!

The hot sweat debacle
Does have its perks –
When you're wrapped up
In duvets and blankets – the works;
I'll be turning the fire down
Stripping off clothes,
Got built in central heating –
And you'll all be froze!

So HURRAH for the flushes
That keep me awake;
And cause me to act
Like I'm a fruit-cake!
THREE CHEERS for the tyre –
(Like I need a spare)
The lack of libido
The sudden chin hair!

PUT YOUR HANDS TOGETHER
IN RAPTUROUS APPLAUSE!
For the change of life –
The MENOPAUSE!

INSTANT GRATIFICATION

Dark and Mysterious
Or Milky and Light;
I am the cure-all
To make you feel right!
If you've been
Dumped by your fella,
Or you just need a fix;
If you're watching the telly
Or sat at the pics.
Just unwrap me and bite;
Or lick with your tongue –
I can last thirty seconds
Or take all night long…
Most women love me
From near and far –
I'm better than Sex;
I'm a Chocolate Bar!

LOVE IS THE DRUG

You take the heat
Out of sunshine,
The wet out of rain.
The fun out of funny,
The thoughts from my brain.
You are woeful and joyless
With no lust for life;
You bring discord and unrest
And sorrow and strife.
Yet I yearn for your presence,
And ache for your touch –
You are my reason;
You are my crutch.
With you I feel pleasure
And pain like no other;
You are my saviour
My brother, my lover.
You are the free-fall –
The speed of light.
You are the voice
In my head late at night.
You are the cure when
Life is insane…
You are the drug that
Pumps through my vein.

MOLE ON THE LEFT BUTTOCK

As we sat and sipped our wine
At 'La Trocador',
I couldn't help but notice
She kept staring at the floor.
'What's up?' I asked a tad concerned,
And as she raised her head –
I wasn't quite prepared
For what she then next said.

She'd been having lots of problems
With her man – Or so it seemed;
He'd been acting out of character
And couldn't be redeemed.
She was sharing her suspicions
With someone who'd sympathise –
She was sick and tired
Of how things were
And putting up with lies!

Recently he'd joined the gym
And lost around three stone;
She saw him preening like a peacock
When he thought he was alone –
He'd bought a new convertible

And if that was not enough –
He'd been spending time in Selfridges
And buying lots of stuff!

He was terrified of needles
So why on earth would he –
Get a tattoo on his leg
That said 'you belong to me'!
The reason must be simple
She said answering her question;
I felt a burning in my chest
The on-set of indigestion…

She cried, 'He's got another woman!'
And started into my eyes;
I felt my stomach lurch
As I began to realise –
The man I met six months ago
Liked going to the gym –
He had a new convertible,
He said his name was 'Tim'…

But I'm sure that's just coincidence
'Cause between me and you
Lots of men out there
Have got the same tattoo!
But does he bite his bottom lip
When he's concentrating?
Or get cross at 'Sunday' drivers
By gesticulating?

Does he sit and stroke your hair?
When you are watching telly?
Or rest his head upon
Your less than perfect belly?
Does he mouth 'I love you'
When he's walking out the room?
Or tell you that he really likes
The smell of your perfume?

'If he does these things' – she said,
'It's clear for all to see –
The man that you are dating
Still belongs to ME!'
I felt like such a FOOL –
I felt so small and meek
When she asked me if he had
A mole on his left buttock cheek…

MY DAD THE LODGER

My poor old Dad
Was frail and weak
Heart of gold
And mild and meek,
So any doubts
Were soothed away;
When I asked him
To come and stay.

A metamorphosis
Then took place
And continued
At alarming pace
My poor old Dad
Once so frail –
Was striving
To be Alpha Male!

I tried hard
Not to go insane
When the kitchen
Became his domain;
And when he was
Taken by the mood –

He'd cook some
Noxious tasting food!

Our garden hardly
Saw the mower
Till Dad turned into
Percy Thrower –
And herbs that I
Had planted new,
Were lost when
Six foot poppies grew!

He'd stay up In
His room for hours
Reading up on
'Special Powers' –
Preparing for the
Huge bombshell –
That he had formed
His own Cartel!

So Dad – It is with
Deep remorse
Before my spouse
And I divorce –
We're leaving
EVERYTHING to you –
And moving out
To pastures new…

PORTION CONTROL

I used to be size eight you know;
Wore nowt but skinny jeans –
But now I fit in size sixteen
And they're busting at the seams!

It's not my fault – It's medical
My thyroid's gone to pot,
And what with that and dodgy knees,
I can't exercise a lot.

I try to live a healthy life –
Follow a diet plan;
But it's really hard to stick to rules,
With an appetite like a man!

I'll be really good tomorrow,
 I'll watch what's on my plate –
So I'll have just one more portion please –
I need to watch my weight!

THE WRONG TROUSERS

I bought some bright pink
Running shoes
This time I would get fit;
So I set off down the road,
Undaunted – full of grit!

I'd only gone a hundred yards
Before I had
The stitch –
I urged myself to carry on,
For this was just a glitch!

I caught sight of
My reflection
In a shop as I trudged past;
Lord knows how I'd managed this
I stared on all aghast.

Instead of
My new trackies –
In the early morning haze;
My reflection caught me wearing
My polar bear PJ's!

PROCRASTINATION

We're bombarded with great pressure
From the point of our conception –
To be successful and achieve
All that we can – with no exception!
Dictated to by Governments
And image from the media;
It's no wonder we're all anxious
And rocking in hysteria!

I'd rather just procrastinate;
Do things in my own time –
To bend the rules a little;
Not always tow the line.
So today I'll take it easy
I might even stay in bed…
There's always time tomorrow –
I'll do it then, instead!

NO SEX IN THE CITY

We're older now
But when we meet
(Despite the bunions on our feet!)
We still can kick our heels about
Bop till we drop
And twist and shout.
It only takes a wine or two
To have us rushing to the loo
But we still go in pairs
Or threes –
To talk about our dodgy knees;
And all you skinny young 'uns there
Fake boobies and your
Coiffured hair;
To us you are no competition –
We're in our prime
And on a mission!
The mission's not
What you would think;
No chasing blokes
Or downing drink
Or other stuff – for goodness sake!
Our mission's just
TO STAY AWAKE!

SALSA

His hips swayed to the rhythm
Of the sexy Latin beat;
I listened to the music
And began to move my feet;
But they refused to listen
They were doing their own thing;
Bouncing off the floor
As though propelled by spring!

How hard could it be? - I thought;
To master this routine –
I was keen, I was able,
I could be a dancing queen!
'You're too stiff' Said his voice
As he grabbed my sweaty hand;
And twirled me round the dance floor
In a movement quite unplanned!

I began to lose my footing
On the seventh pirouette;
I knew dancing with an expert
Would be something I'd regret!
But I painted on a smile
And I flicked my un-tamed hair;

And I mamboed and I shimmied
Like I didn't have a care!

I flung my free arm out –
Ready to turn it up a notch,
And I realised in horror
That I'd whacked him in the crotch!
There were tears in his eyes
As he tried to gain composure;
Pretend it never happened –
Tried to give it closure….

But the whole room was in uproar,
So we didn't get the chance –
To pretend that it was part
Of our own 'Dirty Dance';
So I've reached the conclusion
That Salsa's not for me –
I'm as agile as a hippo
And I've got a dodgy knee….

And just like the nursery rhyme
About the young Jack Horner,
This 'Baby's' bowing out
And staying in the corner!

SEPARATE WORLDS

I see you almost every day
A lonely figure at the station.
Just another commuter
Waiting to board the 5.20 train.
I see you standing there
Staring into space;
Too pre-occupied with your thoughts
To ever notice me.
Occasionally our eyes meet
Momentarily – I imagine you know
How I feel;
And can read the message
Replaying in my mind.
Then you turn away
And I realise that it was
Only wishful thinking...
The train arrives.
Mechanically we clamber on -
Slamming the doors behind.
Both in separate carriages
Both in separate worlds.
Sitting by the window
I gaze out at the passing objects;

But all I see is your face,
As the train speeds off
Into the distance…

SOCIAL MEDIA

Welcome to a place
In cyberspace
Where you can
Really be accepted.
A Utopia for egotists
And hedonists;
Log in and get connected!
With a multitude of friends
That make weekends
Almost bearable to face –
It's your platform
For free speech;
For you to demonstrate
Your very own showcase!
Social media
An encyclopaedia
Of random connotation;
Where sharing banal trivia
Becomes a true vocation.

TANGOTONIN

The hormonal neurotransmitter which dancers secrete in large quantities when enjoying a particularly wonderful dance. While scientists have as yet failed to identify its chemical structure or locate its receptors in the brain, empirical evidence demonstrates that its effects are powerful, dangerous and habit-forming.

He's making her cry again –
Vile words pour out
And evaporate into the ether.
She hears only white noise.
It's taken practise….
She pictures him;
Throat slit
Blood spurting from his jugular
Or with a bullet
Lodged in his head,
Or a noose around his neck –
Like the one
He lassoed her with
The day they first met.
In this moment
She feels helpless

As if trying to escape
The clutches of
A predatory animal.
She wants to run
But she feels paralysed….

Look at his face –
Twisted and gnarled in anger.
He towers above her
With a self-important gait.
Her falling tears
Make him cringe;
They resonate like nails
Raking down a chalkboard.
She knows that
Any second now
He will explode.
His flailing arm approaches
And rests upon
Her unsuspecting face.
The back of his hand
Feels sweet
Against her bare flesh….
She's getting
What she deserves.
It's almost over;
Their dance –
A well-polished Tango.
She topples

Then expertly gains composure,
And stares deep
Into his soulless eyes.
Now he crumbles!
She feels pleased
With this result.
"I'm sorry!" He exclaims
Looking on in disbelief
As if he were a voyeur
At a crash site.
Her face –
All contorted and bruised.
She stands rigid;
Until she feels his arms
Wrap like a boa constrictor
Around her middle…..
And in this moment –
In this moment,
She feels herself
Melt into him;
And they become one again.
'I will never leave'
She thinks out loud.
He knows
She will never leave…….

THE JOURNEY

Objects go whizzing past
Tainted by the rain stained window,
Majestic trees wave as I pass by;
Cows continue to gorge on
The dew covered grass.
Faster and faster we go –
Past stone built cottages
And miles and miles
Of desolate green fields.
This is my life.
I close my eyes and remember
Seeing this beauty
For the first time.
It was never enough.
A void remained.
It grew to gargantuan proportions;
My heart yearned for what was…
Every bone and sinew
Ached to be closer...
Lost in my thoughts
I notice a metamorphosis
Taking place.
Outside the objects
Suddenly look clearer.

Trees have turned into
High rise office towers;
Green meadows into
A maze of tarmac and concrete.
Turning the corner
The huge space-age
Silver bubble covered mecca
That is 'Selfridges' –
Comes into view.
I feel a wave of familiarity
Wash over me –
This feels good!
This feels right!
My heart beats faster,
My bones no longer ache
And the void heals over
As if I've been touched
By some greater being –
I am home again…

It's true what they say
About the colour of grass…

WHAT'S IN A NAME?

The whole school sat in silence
As the Head droned on about;
How important that this day was
To dispel religious doubt.

For on this day an age ago
In a town in France –
Some school-girls saw the
Virgin Mary quite by chance;

And I was waiting patiently
In front of all the hordes
To tell them all how I was named
After a town called 'Lourdes'.

As I stood up my mouth went dry,
My legs began to quake;
There wasn't time to make it up -
They'd soon know I was fake!

I looked around at staring eyes,
The kids began to chant;
I took a breath and then announced –
'um….I was named after me Aunt!'

WHY DON'T YOU LOVE ME?

(For Honey the Dog)

I work hard each and every day
To earn an honest crust;
I rarely let things bother me
But you leave me nonplussed!
When I walk through
That door at night,
Is it too much to expect?
For you to just notice me,
To show me some respect?

Remember without me
You might be homeless – on the streets;
Without that comfy bed of yours
With crisp white cotton sheets;
So you'd better just consider this
The next time I'm around –
Or I might make a phone call
And lock you in the pound!

Why? oh why? does she deserve
The love you've got to give?
I can't try any harder,
I've lost the will to live!
So Honey, show me something –
I'm the one that cleans your crap;

Don't choose her;
Choose me instead!
Now get down off her lap!

THE RESULT

Hurrah we're independent!
We've put the 'Great' back into Britain!
No more EU rule for us -
Our laws will be re-written!
We don't want any foreigners
Tarnishing our land -
We'd rather send them home
And have our hospitals unmanned!

If Scotland leaves, so what?
We don't need them anymore;
And as for Northern Ireland -
Off you go; there's the door!
Like a phoenix from the ashes;
We will rise, wait and see!
We'll be better off alone
We're the new bourgeoisie!

Don't worry about the interest rates
Or the NHS -
Nige and Boris will look after things,
They offer such finesse...
'Calm down' we're English people!
Democracy's our right -

We won the bloody war for you;
Our future's looking bright!

We may be small but we're the best,
So get on board the boat!
I was thinking of the kiddies
When I went to cast my vote!

We need to work as one
So we can stop ourselves from veering -
Just a minute! Fucking hell -
IS THERE ANYBODY STEERING?!

STILL SEARCHING

Why am I still looking for
Something I'll never find?
I tell myself it can't exist –
Yet still it's on my mind.
I try to cope alone with life
Pretend that I'm content –
But it has a hold so strong
The feeling won't relent.
It makes me stay awake at night,
It sometimes makes me cry;
It makes me question life itself –
It makes me want to die,
But – what is this love
They talk about?
This all consuming passion?
Where boy meets girl
And falls in love –
Has it gone out of fashion?
I know that I'll keep searching
And my findings won't be right;
And I'll still regret tomorrow –
The things I did last night;
But the thought that keeps me going

Is the dream that love will be –
Behind the next closed door I find,
And looking out for me…

THE WHEELCHAIR

Shiny and blue
I bought a brand new
Wheelchair for my Dad to sit in –
But he swore when he saw it,
He said he abhorred it –
And wouldn't use that thing
To shit in!

ROAD RAGE

(A homage to Dr John Cooper Clarke)

Fucking women

Fucking trollies

Fucking nobs

With fucking brollies!

Fucking men

On fucking bikes

Fucking Queens

And fucking dykes!

Fucking fatties going slow;

Don't they know

I've got to go!

Fucking blacks

Fucking whites

Stop me at the fucking lights!

Fucking hippies

Fucking punks

Fucking skateboards

Fucking drunks!

Fucking oldies

Fucking scooters

Silly tarts

With fucking hooters!

Fucking teens

On fucking phones

Fucking druggies

Skin and bones!
Fucking beggars
On the street
All that have
Two fucking feet!
I want to fucking
Mow you down –
It's evidently, Dudley Town!

LOOKING BACK

A smile when I'm home in the evening;
A kiss when we climb into bed
Is all the love that I need from you,
Day to day -
She so very often said.

He found it hard to show her his feelings,
Except those of sadness and rage –
And she felt like a delicate bird
That had its wings clipped –
And was caught and trapped in a cage.

Both of them looked for a way out.
She left and came back once or twice;
And they did share some
Good times together –
It hinged on the roll of a dice.

Then one day, without any warning;
They were old – looking back on their time.
When life was less of a challenge –
And they were younger,
And both in their prime.

They thought of the time they had wasted –
When they should have been living care-free;
But instead spent their time
Alienated;
Because they could never agree.

It was too late to dance in the moonlight;
Hold hands and run in the rain.
Their joints were too stiff to remember,
Their bodies –
Now ravaged by pain…

They wished they could re-live the moments;
To change their hand of fate –
They've learnt life goes on by way too quickly;
So - show love
Before it's too late.

JACK

We have a dog
His name is Jack
His fur is long
And sleek and black.
We bought him
He was half the size –
With big brown eyes
That hypnotised.
A ball of fluff
He'd play and hide –
Innocence personified!
But now I swear
Upon his head
A 666 I clearly read!
Twas when he chewed
The lino up
And swallowed most
Of my make-up!
He's just a pup
The experts said –
Healthy, handsome
And pure bred,
Ignore him when
He scrapes the door

And craps upon
The bedroom floor;
I tried my best –
I really did!
A twitch evolved
From my eye-lid!
There seemed no way
You could restrain
This hyperactive hurricane!
We bought toys galore
To pacify –
But when we came
To say 'goodbye' –
He'd only hear the front door shut;
And turn into a possessed mutt!
Now we're joining
An obedience class
Where naughty doggies
Go en masse –
And bad behaviour
Will be quelled –
If he doesn't get
Himself expelled!

IN LOVE

I used to gaze into the sky
And see nothing
But the dark;
I used to walk
Amongst the trees;
And think them
Cold and stark.
I used to sit upon the sand
And never hear the sea;
I used to think that nobody
Would fall in love
With me…

But now the stars
Burn in the sky –
They light the way ahead!
And trees bow down
And shed their leaves –
To carpet where I tread!
And when I sit
Upon the sand –
The sea calls out to me;
And tells me
That I'll feel this way –
For all eternity...

THE VOTE

I stare at the paper
And hope that my cross
Will end all political discourse…
The rich will be poorer
And poor will be richer
And the fat cats
Will show some remorse…
But my little world's
Made of white fluffy clouds
Filled with love
And givers and thankers
So no matter who's picked
It won't change a jot –
They're all a bunch of wankers!

HEAVY METAL

I smelt the sweet patchouli
Mixed with lager and pork crunch;
They were acting quite unruly
This neanderthalian bunch!

A thumping in my chest hurt
As guitars began to squeal –
I was a heavy rock convert
And felt like a fifth-wheel!

Why wasn't I informed
There would be a big stampede?
And my ears would get deformed?
And my brain would surely bleed?

The massive speakers boomed –
The crowd were going crazy –
I felt we were all doomed;
Things became a little hazy.

People jumped around
And I tried not to get hit;
Heads were thrashing to the sound –
I was stuck in a mosh pit!

And in the claustrophobic space
I began to feel the groove;
My heart started to race
And my feet began to move

And I jumped for all I'm worth –
Head-banged with all my might!
It felt like a 're-birth'
It felt like pure delight!

Too soon it was all over
The crowd began dispersing;
Too much booze consumed –
A hangover they'd be nursing.

But my ears could hear a noise –
Like the 'whooshing' of the sea;
And years on it still destroys
The silences for me.

Still I'm really glad I've seen
Heavy Rock's great royalty –
Let me now inform
I offer no disloyalty

MOTORHEAD ARE KING!
And though it makes me cuss –
I'll remember when;
Lem gave me tinnitus!

CROSSED WIRES

You hated change of any kind
In your mind you knew
Exactly how the day
Was going to go –
And I tried to make it so.

I tried to protect from
Anyone or anything
That would infect your rationale;
Your morale –
Was too easy to bruise.

In school you were
Abused – used
By kids who thought
That you were
Acting weird.

They smeared shit
On your clothes
And who knows –
What else
 They put you through.

You hid your pain in art;
You drew everything
You saw and more –
As I tried hard
Not to fall apart…

Growing up
The answers were confusing
Hours were spent
Perusing books;
To help you comprehend.

Sometimes you'd pretend;
So I'd loosen the
Apron strings a bit -
I knew
I had to submit…

The teens bought infatuation –
Agitation.
The opposite sex were not kind;
They didn't understand
Your mind

How a break-up
Would affect you…
And I told you
A hundred texts a day
Was not the way to win a heart.

That was the start.
Now you're a man-
You had
 A master plan
And went to Uni.

You learnt to hide
The ticks;
And other tricks;
So no-one
Knew the difference.

You filled your soul
With music –
Bought a guitar
Taught yourself
To use it.

Life is still not easy
You know it never will be –
Without sounding cheesy,
I think you will agree –
That change is good!

That you could –
Achieve anything you want;
You could!
And while some dreams
May shatter

In the end –
People's differences;
Really
Don't
Matter.

AMNESIA

I thought that I'd forgotten
How it felt to see your face.
The way my body fluttered –
I thought time had erased.

I thought that I'd forgotten
How it felt to hold you near;
To feel your breath against my skin -
Heart loud enough to hear.

I thought that I'd forgotten –
But when we accidently met;
You made me remember
That I don't want to forget.

THE WAY IT IS

The spider spied a little fly
All tangled in his web,
And giving it a long hard poke
Here's what the fly then said
'Spare me Mr spider
'cos I'm too small to be dinner –
Why don't you find a dragonfly
I hear that they're a winner!'

The spider thought a little while
Of what the fly had said,
And leaning over to the fly
He then bit off his head!
Although it sounds a sad sad end
Don't get in a tizz –
You can't change Mother Nature;
It's just the way it is…

A MOMENT OF REALISATION

It moved a fraction.
Metal teeth meeting triumphantly.
Just another few inches
Past the alien flesh –
Dimpled and putrid
That wobbled beneath;
And time would not be to blame
Nor the lifestyle
Of the self-confessed hedonist.

Suddenly – defiantly – selfishly;
It halted.
The alien flesh wept
Under the tight fabric.
Teeth firmly clamped in place
Oblivious to tugging; Pulling;
Coaxing; Cajoling;
Nor squirming this way and that –
Like a fish on the end of a hook.

Once calm air
Now infected with expletives.
Hope turned to despair;
Victory –

To defeat.
The realisation became
All too apparent –
Those jeans,
Were never going to fit again.

TRYING AGAIN

We've been up
We've been down
But we're trying again…

We've gone around
And around
But we're trying again…

We've had fights
We've had rows
But we're trying again…

We remembered
Our vows
So we're trying again…

Made in the USA
Charleston, SC
23 August 2016